Living Legends II
...Six Stories about Incredible Deaf People

by
Darlene Toole

Butte Publications, Inc.
Hillsboro, Oregon

Living Legends II
Six Stories about Incredible Deaf People

by Darlene Toole

Acknowledgments:
Editor: Glenn Williams
Pictures: provided by the subjects, used by permission.
Cover design and Layout: Anita Jones

Note: A percentage of the proceeds will be donated to **Infant Hearing Resource (IHR)**, a department of the Hearing and Speech Institute (HSI) located in Portland, Oregon.

IHR serves deaf and hard-of-hearing children, from infancy to four, as well as their their families. At IHR, all forms of communication are encouraged.

Butte Publications, Inc.
P.O. Box 1328
Hillsboro, OR 97123-1328
U.S.A.

ISBN: 1-884362-32-X

Table of Contents

*Dedication: In memory of Anne Sullivan
and teachers
who dedicate their lives
to deaf children*

and

*my friend,
Ray L. Jones*

Thomas Hopkins Gallaudet and Alice Cogswell

"Life is either a daring adventure or nothing."

— HELEN KELLER

Introduction
(To the Teacher)

Living Legends 2, like the first volume of Living Legends, is a book of six stories about deaf people who have displayed courageous effort in achieving excellence in their chosen vocations or avocations.

At the beginning of each story there is a word list with simple definitions to help students understand some vocabulary words that will be used in the story.

Several stories include an expanded activity or fact sheet called **The More You Know**.

At the end of each story are comprehension questions. These questions can be used to test the student's understanding individually or with a group.

A creative writing exercise also follows each story. Encourage students to create their own paragraphs or stories to help develop their writing skills.

How To Use This Book

This book contains six stories. Each story has a vocabulary introduction page and two different exercises.

Words to Know - Vocabulary Introduction Page
Before each story there are vocabulary words with simple definitions. Study these words before you read the story. Discuss these words with your teacher.

Stories
Read each story carefully. Check the words you do not know on the vocabulary introduction page.

The More You Know
After some of the stories, there is a fun fact sheet or an activity that will help you understand the story better. Discuss these with your teachers and classmates.

Check Your Understanding Exercise
At the end of each story there are some comprehension questions that will help you remember what you read. Discuss your answers with your teacher and classmates.

Write About Exercise
This exercise will help you develop better writing skills. Share your paragraphs and stories with your teacher and classmates.

Danny Delcambre:
Words to Know

chef	the head cook of a restaurant
gumbo	a soup-like dish
jambalaya	a Cajun dish of black-eyed peas and Polish sausage cooked in a spicy broth and rice
tasty	delicious; tasting good
to prepare	to fix; to make
popular	well-liked
"The Emerald City"	Seattle, Washington
Cajun	a French speaking group of people who settled in a part of Louisiana
customer	a person who buys something
traditional	customary; passed on from parents to their children
Usher's Syndrome	a hereditary condition that causes a person to be deaf and legally blind
	Fact: 1% of the deaf population in the United States has Usher's Syndrome, yet 10% of the deaf population in Louisiana has Usher's Syndrome

1

hereditary	passed on from an ancestor or relative
Seattle Central Community College (SCCC)	a college in Seattle, Washington which offers deaf students support services, such as interpreters, note-takers, special classes, etc.
supportive	helpful
career	the work a person chooses to do in life
machinist	a person who makes tools and special parts for machines
intern	a person who is learning how to do a job by doing it; a trainee or an apprentice
cuisine	a way of fixing food
Small Business Administration	a federal agency that oversees small businesses such as restaurants, shops, etc.
employees	workers

Danny Delcambre:
The Ragin Cajun

Ask **chef** Danny Delcambre, "What's cooking?" and he'll tell you: **gumbo, jambalaya**, crawdads, and catfish. These **tasty** dishes are all **prepared** by Danny at his famous restaurant, Ragin Cajun in Seattle, Washington.

Danny's restaurant is located at Pike's Place Market in downtown Seattle. It is a **popular** place that has many restaurants and shops.

People come from all over the world to visit Seattle, **"The Emerald City."** Chef Delcambre has served his special **Cajun** food to people from many different countries such as Russia, Denmark, and Germany. Danny's most famous **customer** in 1995 was President Bill Clinton!

Danny Delcambre was born in New Iberia, Louisiana, which is the home of Tabasco sauce. People use Tabasco sauce to add spice and flavor to all kinds of food, but especially to Cajun food.

Danny is from a very **traditional** Cajun family. People with Cajun backgrounds are French and their families settled in part of Louisiana known as Acadiana. Danny says, "My parents cooked Cajun food all the time when I was growing up, and I learned a lot from watching my mother cook."

Some of Danny's favorite Cajun dishes are:

Jambalaya — black-eyed peas and Polish sausage cooked in spicy broth and rice

Gumbo — a soup-like dish made with chicken, shrimp or sausage over rice

Red Beans & Rice with Andouille — Cajun sausage cooked with red beans and rice

Danny is the only deaf and blind chef to own a restaurant in the United States. He and his older sister were born with **Usher's Syndrome.** This is a **hereditary** condition that caused him to be born both deaf and legally blind. He cannot drive a car or see anything that isn't directly in front of him. He might lose all of his sight some day. He explains, "Each person who has Usher's Syndrome has their own problems. I don't know when I will be totally blind.

4

It isn't as if you lose all of your vision and everything becomes black. It's more like a camera going out of focus. Everything gets cloudy and white."

When Danny Delcambre was growing up in Louisiana, he attended the Louisiana State School for the Deaf in Baton Rouge. He stayed there from the age of five to the age of eighteen. After he graduated from school in 1980, he worked at a McDonald's restaurant for five years. He cleaned tables and fried hamburgers. He worked at other jobs as well, until 1987, when he decided to move to Seattle and attend **Seattle Central Community College**.

Why did Danny move so far away from home? He found out that the Seattle area had a very **supportive** deaf and blind community. He also learned that it was a good place to live because Seattle offered many jobs, housing opportunities and outdoor activities.

After he settled in "The Emerald City," he needed to focus on a **career**. Danny decided to take classes at Seattle Central Community College. At first, he studied to be a **machinist**. He got a job working in a machine shop that hired blind workers. Then he decided to change his career plans. He took several cooking classes at SCCC and enjoyed himself so much that he decided to become a chef.

In 1992, Danny wanted to find work as a chef in a restaurant, but he couldn't find a job. He became upset and said, "I applied for jobs several times and it's been real frustrating. People refuse to hire me because I am deaf and blind."

Luckily, he didn't give up because soon a

famous Louisiana chef named Paul Prudhomme gave Danny a chance to work at his restaurant, K Paul's Louisiana Kitchen in New Orleans. Danny worked there as an **intern** chef for two and a half months. He had an interpreter and was able to learn a lot about cooking Cajun **cuisine** and about running a restaurant. Finally in 1993, Chef Delcambre's dream came true. He worked with the **Small Business Administration** and got a bank loan. He was able to start his own restaurant, Ragin Cajun.

What makes a successful restaurant? Danny thinks it is important to serve good fresh food, to have good service and to be a fun place to eat. Chef Delcambre has both deaf and hearing workers in the restaurant. He thinks good communication is important, so all his **employees** use sign language.

Danny has won several awards. He was awarded "Small Business Employer of the Year" from the State of Washington in 1994. His restaurant was chosen "Small Business of the Year" by the City of Seattle in the same year. He has been seen on local and national television. When he isn't cooking and winning awards, he enjoys spending time with his wife, Holly. He also loves horseback riding and skiing.

Brave. Creative. Successful. These are words that describe Danny Delcambre. In the future, he hopes to share his experiences with other people. He says, "I hope to give speeches about how people with disabilities can succeed. I have a lot of things to share with people."

Check Your Understanding

1. When did Danny move to Seattle?

2. How did Danny feel when he couldn't find a job as a chef?

3. What are some different kinds of food found in Cajun dishes?

4. Where do Danny and his wife Holly live now?

5. Who did Danny watch cook when he was a young boy?

6. How do you know that Danny is a successful chef?

Write About

What is your favorite kind of food? Chinese? Italian? Cajun? Mexican? Tell about some of your favorite dishes.

Kathy Buckley:
Words to Know

comedian	a person who makes people laugh; a comic
to nominate	to chose a person
professional	paid to do something
"stand-up" comic	a person who stands in front of an audience to tell jokes
humor	the funny part of something
attitudes	feelings about someone or something
disabilities	barriers to overcome

Example: blindness, deafness, etc. |
spinal meningitis	a disease that causes a person to have chills, and a high fever
dyslexic	a learning problem that makes reading and writing difficult
accent	a way of pronouncing words
warehouse	a building where things are stored
aerobics	exercises that help the body take in and use more oxygen

massage therapist	a person who rubs muscles and joints of the body
fashion designer	a person who draws or designs clothes
contest	a competition; something you try to win
to soar	to go very high
appearances	performances in front of people
sitcom	a weekly situation comedy show on television
role models	people you look up to and admire

Kathy Buckley:
Funny Lady

Comedian Kathy Buckley says with a big smile, "I really like making people laugh and feel good inside. I want people to come into my world so we can laugh together. I like feeling the laughter."

In 1995, Kathy became the first hearing impaired comedian to be **nominated** for an American Comedy Award. In 1996 and also in 1997, she was nominated again! She is a **professional "stand-up" comic** with a great sense of **humor**. She says, "Humor is the best and most harmless way to teach people anything."

What does Kathy joke about? She laughs at

her own problems that come from havng a hearing loss. She also tries to change other people's feelings about deafness. She teaches people through her humor about having the right **attitudes** toward **disabilities**. Her message is: "You can do anything when the heart and mind work together."

Kathy never dreamed she would become a famous comedian when she was growing up in Wickliffe, Ohio. Doctors don't know if she was born with a hearing loss or lost her hearing from **spinal meningitis**. She didn't talk and couldn't understand other people. Her parents and teachers thought she was slow and lazy.

Kathy was put in a special school for retarded children for two years. Finally, after she was given several medical tests, doctors discovered that she had a hearing loss and was **dyslexic**. She went to a public school and worked on her speech and lipreading skills.

For thirteen years, she went to special speech classes. Now when she talks people think she's from New York. Kathy laughs, "I don't get it! How did I get a New York **accent**?" In 1972, she graduated from Wickliffe High School.

Sadly, Kathy experienced two unlucky accidents after she graduated from high school. First, she was in a terrible car accident. She was badly injured and got 32 stitches in her face.

A few years later, bad luck struck again. Kathy was sunbathing on a beach in Ohio. She didn't hear a jeep drive by. Suddenly, she was run over by a 3,500 pound lifeguard jeep. It ran over her chest, shoulders, stomach, face and back. She was in and out of the hospital for five years, and she spent time in and out of a wheelchair, too. Her doctors told her that she would never walk again. Kathy says she didn't hear them, so she got up and walked off!

She decided to move to California when she was twenty-seven years old. She had no place to live in California, so she lived out of her car for two months. Later, she got a job and found an apartment.

But bad luck seemed to follow Kathy. Just when she got settled, she got cancer. Again she was in and out of the hospital for two years. Luckily, she recovered and is now free of cancer.

Kathy Buckley has had many different jobs. She's been a **warehouse** manager, a model, an actress, an **aerobics** teacher, a **massage therapist**, and a **fashion designer**. Whatever job she had, she enjoyed making people laugh.

In 1988, a good friend encouraged Kathy to enter a comedian **contest** in Los Angeles. Eighty people entered the competition, and Kathy earned fourth place. Since then, her career as a comedian has **soared**.

For many years, whenever Kathy performed, she couldn't hear people laugh at her jokes. Finally, she was able to get two powerful hearing aids that helped her hear some sounds. The first time she heard people laugh at her jokes she cried and cried, because she was so happy.

Kathy has performed at some of the most popular comedy clubs in the United States. She has also performed at the Kennedy Center in Washington DC.

Her many television **appearances** include: *Live with Regis and Kathy Lee, Entertainment Tonight* and the *American Comedy Awards.*

When Kathy Buckley was growing up, she hated coping with her deafness. Sometimes being hearing impaired and being misunderstood made her frustrated and angry. Now she considers her hearing loss and life a gift. She says, "No matter how hard your life gets, it's only for the moment. You have to make the best of each moment and enjoy it for what it is."

Kathy's future plans are clear. She would love to star in her own **TV sitcom**. She would also like to continue acting, telling jokes, and speaking to all kinds of people with disabilities. She especially wants to reach out to children. She explains, "Children should have healthy **role models** to show them that people do care about them deeply."

This tall, funny and talented comedian proves that dreams come true if you believe in yourself and never give up.

The More You Know

Many deaf and hard of hearing women have won awards in the entertainment world. Here are a few of them.

Entertainer	Award	Category	Year
Phyllis Frelich	"Tony"	Best Actress in a Broadway Play: *Children of a Lesser God*	1980
Linda Bove	"Emmy"	Best Actress in a Television Show: *Sesame Street*	
Mary Lou Novitsky	"Emmy"	Co-Producer & Co-host of a TV Show: *Deaf Mosaic*	(5 times)
Juliana Fjeld	"Emmy"	Best Producer of a TV Movie: *Love is Never Silent*	1986
Marlee Matlin	"Oscar" & Golden Globe	Best Actress in a Motion Picture: *Children of a Lesser God*	1987
Evelyn Glennie	"Grammy"	Best Musician in a Recording: *Bartok's Sonata for Two Pianos and Percussion*	1989

| Kathy Buckley | "Emmy" | Producer & Actress in Best Documentary Film: *Heart of the Nation (I Can Hear the Laughter)* | 1991 |
| | "Ovation" | Producer & Writer One Woman Show: *Don't Buck with Me!* | 1997 |

Awards in Entertainment

"Emmy" Award	a special television award
"Grammy" Award	a special music award
Golden Globe Award	a special award given by the foreign press
"Tony" Award	a special theatre award N.Y.
"Oscar" or Academy Award	a special movie award
"Ovation Award"	a special theatre award L.A.

Check Your Understanding

1. Why do you think Kathy tells jokes about herself?

2. Where does she perform her stand-up comedy?

3. When did Kathy graduate from high school?

4. How did Kathy end up in a wheelchair?

5. What are Kathy's future plans?

6. Why do you think Kathy uses humor to teach others about people with disabilities?

Write About

What is your favorite sitcom on television? Explain who is in the show and why you like it.

Ken Glickman:
Words to Know

"jinxoes" — the white boxes often found in garbled TV captions

"oopstacle" — anything that a walking Deafie bumps into while talking to another Deafie

"superchat" — to carry on a conversation through a huge storefront window at a supermarket

a.k.a. — also known as

Example: Ken Glickman, a.k.a. "Prof. Glick"

"Prof. Glick" — nickname for Professor Glickman in his comedy show, DEAFology 101

author — a person who writes books, stories, etc.

publisher — a person or company that publishes books, magazines, etc.

"Signlets" — new words or phrases that explain things about deaf people and their culture

serious — not funny; solemn

awkward — uncomfortable

"Hearie"	a hearing person
"Deafie"	a deaf person
bearable	acceptable; tolerable
hereditary	passed on from an ancestor or relative
valedictorian	a top honor student
Psychology	the study of the mind and the way people and animals behave
adventure	an exciting experience
patient	tolerant; considerate
IBM	a nickname for the company, International Business Machines
computer programmer	a person who writes programs for computers
Faculty Loan Program	a program where employees from a company volunteer to teach at schools and colleges
computer graphics	making pictures and designs using a computer
viewpoint	observation opinion

Ken Glickman: "Prof. Glick"

"**Jinxoes**"… "**oopstacle**"… "**superchat**"… are these words from another planet?? Ask Ken Glickman, **a.k.a. "Prof. Glick,"** and he will tell you, "None of these words are in the dictionary, but they should be."

Ken is the **author** and **publisher** of two interesting books: *DEAFinitions for Signlets and More DEAFinitions!* "**Signlets**" are new words or phrases about deaf people and their culture. Ken and others created and collected them.

Signlets can be funny. They can also be serious because they show how **awkward** life can sometimes be for deaf and hearing people.

Ken wrote both books for **"Hearies"** and **"Deafies."** He thinks his DEAFinitions will help deaf people share their feelings about deafness. He also feels that his books will help hearing people understand the deaf experience. He says, "Humor makes things **bearable**. It makes the world go 'round."

Ken Glickman was born in Massachusetts in 1953. Both he and his sister were born deaf. They have **hereditary** deafness.

At the age of four and a half, Ken went to the Clarke School for the Deaf in Northampton, Massachusetts. Clarke School for the Deaf is a well-known oral school. Children are taught to use speech and lipreading skills. They do not use sign language. Ken stayed at Clarke School until the eighth grade. After that, he attended a private school called Pine Cobble School. He graduated **valedictorian**.

Ken attended high school at Williston-Northampton School. The only way he could get good grades was to read everything. He did not have an interpreter. He had to copy notes from his classmates. He studied hard and became an honor student. At graduation in 1973, Ken got awards in both chemistry and math.

At the age of twenty, he attended Dartmouth College in Hanover, New Hampshire. He graduated in 1977 with top honors in **psychology** and math.

Before graduating from college, Ken and his roommate took a break from studies and went on an **adventure**. They went to Europe for five months. Ken was able to visit a school for the deaf in

Denmark. He also toured Norway and Sweden and all the way south to Morocco and Israel.

Ken loved Europe. He says, "I would love to go back to Europe. It was much easier being deaf there. People thought I was a German trying to speak English. They were very **patient** and understanding." While in Israel, he had a very funny experience. He and his college roommate were walking around in Jerusalem one day. They saw two women standing across on a street corner. Ken thought one of the women was deaf. His roommate couldn't believe it. So, they both walked over to find out. True enough, Ken was right! The younger woman was deaf and the older woman was her mother. When the older woman found out that Ken was both deaf and Jewish, she wanted him to marry her daughter. Ken laughed, "We got out of there as fast as we could!"

Ken got a job working at **IBM** after graduating from Dartmouth. He was a **computer programmer** and worked at IBM for ten years.

IBM has a special program called a **Faculty Loan Program**. Ken was able to go to Gallaudet University and National Technical Institute for the Deaf. He taught deaf students computer programming and **computer graphics**. His students raved about him. One student said, "He has a special kind of magic that helps deaf people understand. Ken knows we live in pictures, not in words. He shows us that deaf people can do anything."

Ken understands about magic because he is a skilled magician. At the age of twenty-two, he learned two important skills. First he learned sign language. Then he learned how to do magic tricks. With practice, Ken became an expert magician. He even won contests in Europe. He enjoys competing in different shows. Ken also performs for schools, clubs and organizations.

Ken uses the language of magic when he teaches, as well. He explains, "Magic makes teaching more interesting. I might tell the students, 'I have a trick up my sleeve' when I show them how to solve a hard math problem. Also, I might say that a computer program has worked 'like magic.'"

"Prof. Glick" now lives in Silver Spring, Maryland. He owns his own company called DEAFinitely Yours Studio. He creates and sells books, posters, postcards, and a special videotape called DEAFology 101. In this funny video, Ken acts like a professor giving a crazy, crash course on Deaf culture and shows what it is like from a comedian's **viewpoint**.

Creating… imagining… sharing… dreaming… that's Ken. He always seems to have a magic trick up his sleeve!

SUPERCHAT
(SOO per chat)

v. To carry on a leisurely conversation through the huge storefront window at a supermarket.

Ken Glickman, DEAFinitions for Signlets (Maryland: 1986)

24

The More You Know

This is an example of a Signlet from Ken Glickman's book *DEAFinitions for Signlets.*

OOPSTACLE
(OOPS stuh kul)

n. Anything that a walking **DEAFIE** bumps into, especially when deep in **RETRO-STROLLING** with another person.

Define and draw your own Signlet in the space below.

Check Your Understanding

1. How long did Ken work at IBM?

2. List some of the countries that Ken and his roommate visited.

3. Where does Ken live now?

4. What are some of Ken's hobbies?

5. Why do you think Ken wanted to have his own company?

6. When did Ken graduate from college?

Write About

If you could go to Europe, which country would you want to visit the most? Explain why.

Bethany "Buffy" Hummel:
Words to Know

to rank   to put into position or place

Example: first place, second place, etc.

to feature   to show; to star

pioneer   a person who is the first to explore and settle in a place

coach   a teacher or trainer of athletes

to amaze   to surprise

to discover   to find out

local   a nearby place

community   an area where people work and live together

private   not public; something that belongs to a person or group

pastor   a minister in charge of a church

to mainstream   to attend regular classes in a public school with or without support services (such as interpreters, note-takers, etc.)

to enroll   to join

assistant	a helper Example: assistant coach or assistant manager
"driving to the hoop"	quickly moving the ball close to the backboard and up through the hoop to score
"shooting from the outside"	throwing the ball through the hoop from beyond the inside court, close to the backboard
ability	skill
point guard	the player who brings the basketball down the court and sets up a play
to impress	to feel strongly
varsity	the main team
a starter	one of the five starting players on a basketball team
competition	trying to win
scholarship	money that is given to a student to help pay for school or college

Bethany "Buffy" Hummel: The Pioneer

The Dream Team. They were ranked #1 in the nation in 1997 by *USA Today*. They were undefeated (26-0), two years in a row. They were featured in *Sports Illustrated* and on CBS News. They got their picture on a box of Cheerios. The Chicago Bulls? Nope. The Oregon City High School's girl basketball team from Oregon City, Oregon. Home of the **Pioneers**.

This famous "dream team" has won the National Girl's High School Championships three years in a row (1995-97). They have won the Oregon 4A State Championship five years in a row (1994-98). Their string of wins numbers 68-0, a state record!

Their **coach** Brad Smith received the National Girl's High School "Coach of the Year" award in 1997. He says, "It's like a dream come true. It's fantastic. If a person had told me this, I wouldn't have believed it!"

When Bethany "Buffy" Hummel was a child, she never dreamed she would play basketball for a championship team. Buffy is a true pioneer because she is the first deaf player to play for the Oregon City High School's girl's basketball team. What makes her even more **amazing** is that she made the team as a freshman when she was only fourteen years old.

Born deaf from an unknown cause, Buffy was sixteen months old before her parents **discovered** that she was profoundly deaf. Right away, her mother decided to take sign language classes at a **local community** college. She learned quickly and taught Buffy's dad and her older brother, Jonathan. Buffy had clear communication early in her life. Today she uses both her speech and signs.

Until the eighth grade, Buffy attended a **private** church school at Portland Victory Fellowship in Portland, where her father is the **pastor**. Her parents paid for Buffy's interpreter, and she was **mainstreamed** with hearing children. Then the Hummel family moved to Oregon City in 1994. Buffy **enrolled** at Ogden Middle School where she got more involved with basketball.

How did Buffy become such a good basketball player? When she was nine years old, she started playing with her brother. He taught her a lot about the game. They shot "hoops" outside her home, rain or shine. In the fifth grade, Buffy started playing community basketball. Her dad was her **assistant** coach, and her mom became her biggest fan.

Buffy worked hard to improve her game and became a skilled player. Her best skills would later become **driving to the hoop, shooting from the outside**, and **passing the ball**. She had the natural **ability** to be a **point guard** for her team. One of her coaches said, "She is a quick learner, and she always gives 100 percent."

While at Ogden Middle School, Buffy was invited to attend the open gym basketball practices at Oregon City High School (OCHS). When Coach Smith saw her play, he was very **impressed**. He told others, "She is outstanding. She is a great ball handler. She is even better because she has to communicate by watching others."

As a freshman at OCHS, Buffy made the **varsity** team. Even though she wasn't a **starter**, she got to play with some of the best players in the nation. Next year, she will work even harder to be a starter for her team. She says, "The **competition** is tough, but with hard work, I know I can do it."

Being the only deaf student at OCHS doesn't bother Buffy. She explains, "I've been deaf all my life, so I'm used to it. I never really understood what it meant to be deaf, I just grew up with it." At OCHS, Buffy is an excellent student and her favorite subjects are math and P.E. Other sports that she enjoys are track and softball.

Buffy Hummel's future goals are clear. She wants to play varsity basketball for three more years at OCHS. She also wants to help her team with three more State Championships! After graduation, she hopes to get a college **scholarship** to a school like the University of Tennessee. Then her dream is to play professional basketball for either the WNBA (Women's National Basketball Association) or the ABL (American Basketball League). She says, "If you think you want to do sports, you should keep working at it; never give up!"

The More You Know

Buffy's favorites are on the left. Write your
favorites in the blank.

Grapefruit	Food	_____
Math	Subject	_____
Purple	Color	_____
"The X-Files"	TV Show	_____
Sandra Bullock	Actress	_____
Tommy Lee Jones	Actor	_____
"Scream"	Movie	_____
Computer	Hobby	_____
Basketball	Sport	_____
Mexico	Place	_____
"Sprite"	Drink/Soda	_____
"Jeep"	Car	_____

Check Your Understanding

1. Who taught Buffy to play basketball when she was only nine years old?

2. Where does Buffy's family live?

3. How old was Buffy when she made the varsity basketball team at Oregon City High School?

4. Why do you think she wants to attend a college like the University of Tennessee?

5. When was Buffy's team ranked #1 in the nation?

6. Who learned sign language first in the Hummel family?

Write About

What is your favorite sport? Would you want to be a professional athlete? Explain why or why not.

Robert Davila:
Words to Know

diplomat a person from one government who works carefully with another government; a person who works well with other people

migrant worker a farm worker who moves from place to place to pick fruits and vegetables

responsibility duty; work

orchard a group of fruit trees

canvas a strong cloth used to make tents and sails

to survive to live

to discover to find out

serious dangerous

shelter a place that covers and protects you; a home

California School for the Deaf, Berkeley A school begun in 1860. The school campus moved to Fremont, California in 1980. The school is now called California School for the Deaf, Fremont.

native language the language you are born to use

role models	people you respect and admire
Hispanic	people of Mexican and Spanish descent
a whiz	a very smart person
civil engineer	a person who helps design and build bridges and roads
administrator	a person who is responsible for an office or school
dean	a person responsible for students and teachers
headmaster	the principal of a private school
legislators	people who make or pass laws

Robert Davila: The Diplomat

Photo by A. Sue Weisler

When Robert Davila was a young boy, he traveled a lot with his family. He traveled up and down California. His parents were Mexican **migrant workers** from San Diego. They worked on different farms picking fruits and vegetables. They were often hungry and tired. It was a hard life.

Robert's family was poor, but they were rich in love. His parents were hard-working people. They taught Robert and his seven brothers and sisters about work and **responsibility**. All of the Davila children worked hard, helping their parents in the fields and **orchards**.

When Robert was six years old, his father died. One day, Robert and his family spread a **canvas** under a fruit tree. Robert says, "My father climbed the tree to shake it. The fruit fell on the canvas, and we put it in boxes. My father suddenly fell out of the tree, because he had a heart attack. He died. He was only 38 years old."

Robert's family was very sad. His mother had to support eight children alone. She did not have a lot of education. Her skills were limited. It was a very difficult time for the Davila family. But his mother was strong; she would not give up. She worked hard and somehow the family **survived**.

When Robert was eight, he became very sick. His mother thought he had the flu. Robert became weaker and weaker. Finally, his mother called a doctor. The doctor **discovered** that Robert had spinal meningitis. This is a very serious disease that had to be treated right away in the hospital.

Robert was lucky. He survived and his health improved, but the disease destroyed the nerve cells inside his inner ear. Robert realized he was deaf when he woke up one morning in the hospital. He was watching cars outside his window. The cars were quiet. He could hear no noise.

Then, his family came to visit him. They talked to him. They moved their lips, but there were no sounds. At first, Robert thought his brothers were trying to tease him by playing a game. Later, he realized that he couldn't hear them. He knew that he would never hear their voices again.

The Davila family was not very upset about

Robert's deafness. They were happy he was alive and getting stronger. Robert explains, "In my family, **shelter** and food were very important; hearing was not a big deal."

After Robert returned home from the hospital, some friends told his mother about a school for deaf children in Berkeley, California. This school was a long way from Robert's home in San Diego. His mother had to make a decision. Should she let eight year old Robert go to **California School for the Deaf, Berkeley** (CSDB) or should he stay in San Diego?

The Davila family decided that it would be best for Robert to go north to CSDB. True, it was a long way from home, but it would be best for Robert's future.

Robert said, "My life improved because I became deaf. Berkeley's School for the Deaf was a beautiful school with young people who were deaf like I was. Wow! It opened the doorway to a new life better than the one I had before."

At first it was not easy for Robert at CSDB. His **native language** was Spanish. He had to learn two different languages, English and sign language, at the same time. Robert was very smart. He loved learning more than anything and became an outstanding student at CSDB.

During summer vacations, he was able to return home to San Diego, but he spent a lot of time alone. This was not a bad experience for Robert. Being alone taught him to be more independent and self-confident. He has always been close to his family and feels much love for his brothers and sisters.

Children need role models. It is important to have people to admire and respect. It is important to have people encourage your hopes and dreams. Robert was **Hispanic** and deaf. He felt he had few role models growing up. One person he did admire was the famous Hispanic tennis pro named Pancho Gonzales. Robert became a very skilled tennis player and always looked up to Pancho. He admired some of his teachers at CSDB, but they were not Hispanic role models.

Once a teacher asked Robert and his classmates, "What do you want to be when you grow up?" Robert thought about his question. A boy sitting next to him said, "I want to be a teacher." Robert signed and shouted, "I want to be a teacher, too!" Robert's teacher was surprised. He told Robert, "I don't know any Hispanic teachers. I'm not sure it's a good idea."

Instead of giving up and changing his goal in life, Robert met the challenge. He says, "You challenge me, and I'll meet your challenge!" Years later, Robert became a teacher of deaf children and the president of three national organizations in education!

After graduating from CSDB at the age of fifteen, Robert went to Gallaudet College. He was a whiz in math and social studies. He became a very popular student on campus and he was a great leader. He worked part-time at different jobs to earn money to support himself. He even went to different parks in the city to collect soda pop cans to earn extra money. It was not easy going to college and working, but Robert had no choice.

For a while, he thought about becoming a **civil engineer**. He wanted to build bridges and roads. Teachers at Gallaudet did not encourage Robert to major in engineering because at that time, in the 1950's, there were no deaf people in the field. Instead, his teachers encouraged him to become a teacher. They felt it was a good profession for him. Robert agreed and received his B.S. (Bachelor of Science) degree in education.

Robert Davila got his first job at the New York School for the Deaf (NYSD), in White Plains, New York. He taught his favorite subjects: math and social studies. He taught at NYSD for fourteen years.

In 1967, Robert made a change. He wanted to be an **administrator**. He continued to work full-time, but went back to college to get his M.S. (Master of Science) degree in special education, at Hunter College in New York.

He became a supervisor at the New York School for the Deaf. He also continued to go to college and got his Ph.D. (Doctor of Philosophy) degree, at Syracuse University. He became the first deaf Hispanic person to earn a Ph.D. degree in the United States.

In 1974, Dr. Davila became director of Kendall Demonstration Elementary School, at Gallaudet University in Washington DC. For the next fifteen years, Robert held many different jobs. He was a dean, a professor, and the vice-president of Pre-College Programs.

In 1988, George Bush was elected President of the United States. The Republican National

Committee asked Robert if he wanted to become the Assistant Secretary of Special Education and Rehabilitative Services, for the US Department of Education. Dr. Davila said, "Yes!"

Some people did not want Robert to get this important job. Some people felt he was not skilled and experienced. Some people thought that since Robert was deaf, he could not understand about other disabilities. The White House did not agree with these people. The White House supported Robert.

In 1989, Dr. Robert Davila became the Assistant Secretary for Special Education and Rehabilitation Services. He was given the highest government job ever offered to a deaf person. Robert had a big responsibility. He had to work with an annual budget of $5,000,000,000 dollars! He had to direct programs for over 43,000,000 disabled persons and their families. It's a good thing that Robert was a whiz in math!

When Bill Clinton, a Democrat, was elected President of the United States in 1992, Robert had to change jobs. He went back to his former school, New York School for the Deaf, and became its headmaster. As **headmaster**, he made many good changes and improved the spirit of the school. He was respected by all teachers, parents and students.

In 1996, Dr. Davila was offered a job as a vice president of the Rochester Institute of Technology (RIT) with specific responsibility to manage the National Technical Institute for the Deaf (NTID), one of seven colleges of RIT. NTID, which is in Rochester, New York, is the largest technological

college for the deaf in the world. He became the first deaf director in the 29 year history of NTID. When he is not busy supervising the program at NTID, he visits other college programs all over the world. He also speaks to **legislators** in Washington DC.

Robert Davila says about his remarkable life, "It comes down to this: you've got to accept me for what I am — my language, my culture, habits and opinions. If you can't accept me for that, then don't accept me, period. It has to be all the way or not at all."

Robert lives in Pittsford, New York, with his lovely wife, Donna. They have two grown sons who became civil engineers. When Robert has free time, he enjoys spending time with his family, traveling, reading and playing tennis and golf.

Check Your Understanding

1. What happened to Robert at the age of eight that changed his life?

2. How old was Robert when he attended Gallaudet University?

3. Why was life at California School for the Deaf, Berkeley, better for Robert?

4. What are some of Robert's achievements?

5. Where do Robert and his wife live now?

6. If Robert had not lost his hearing, what kind of work do you think he would have chosen to do?

Write About

Dr. Robert Davila has worked at two major universities for deaf students. He has worked at Gallaudet University in Washington DC, and he now works at the National Technical Institute for the Deaf in Rochester, New York. Where would you like to attend college when you graduate from high school? Explain where and why.

Laurene Gallimore:
Words to Know

challenge	a special effort to do something
punishment	a penalty for a crime or wrong; bad treatment
to frustrate	to make someone feel helpless; to discourage
profoundly deaf	a deep and serious hearing loss
to rely	to depend upon; to trust
role models	people you admire and respect
elementary grades	kindergarten through fifth grade, for children ages five to twelve years old
to support	to encourage; to help
bilingual education	using two languages and cultures to teach children Example: ASL and English, Spanish and English, etc.
culture	the arts, beliefs and customs that make up the way of life for a group of people
Ph.D.	Doctor of Philosophy
trainer	a person who helps people learn how to do something

principal	a person who is the head or director of a school
advocate	a person who helps you; a supporter
major	bigger or more important
abuse	to go very high
peer pressure	to use in a way that is bad or wrong
vision	a dream; the ability to plan ahead
hobbies	free-time activities
Example: painting, reading, swimming, etc.
classic	famous and loved by many people

Laurene Gallimore: The Challenge

"Being deaf should be a **challenge**," says Laurene Gallimore, "not a **punishment**."

When Laurene was a child, she was not allowed to use sign language in school. She sat on her hands. If she used signs, her teachers punished her. They slapped her hands with a ruler.

Laurene remembers this terrible experience. She explains, "I cried. I was so **frustrated** in school. The teachers didn't use sign language. It wasn't good for me. I am **profoundly deaf** and rely on my eyes."

Laurene and her classmates found ways to communicate with each other. They used signs behind their teachers' backs. They also used signs outside school time. Sometimes they made up their own signs. They did not have deaf teachers who signed in the **elementary grades**. They did not have good **role models**.

Laurene's early school experience made an important difference in her life. She wanted to change education for other deaf children. Her goal was to become a teacher. Now she is making her dreams come true by helping change how deaf children are educated.

Laurene attended Indiana School for the Deaf. When she was a child, Indiana School for the Deaf did not allow signing in the elementary classes. Slowly, the school changed its way of educating deaf children. Other schools in the United States changed, too. Indiana School for the Deaf is now one of the best schools for deaf children in our country. The school supports **bilingual education**. What is bilingual education?

BILINGUAL EDUCATION
American Sign Language (ASL) & English
Deaf **Culture** & American Culture
Deaf History & American History
Deaf Role Models & Hearing Role Models

After Laurene graduated from Indiana School for the Deaf in 1972, she attended California State University, Northridge for two years. Later she went to the University of Nebraska in Lincoln. She studied very hard and got her degree in elementary education in 1986. Then Laurene attended Western Maryland

College in Westminster, Maryland. She got her **M.Ed.** (Masters in Education) in 1987.

She has had many different jobs. She has been a teacher, an interpreter trainer, a **principal**, an author, and an **advocate** for deaf children. In 1995, Laurene and her family moved to Oregon. She got a job at Western Oregon University (WOU) in Monmouth, Oregon. She trains people to become teachers of deaf children.

When she first started working at WOU, she said, "I was in for a shock, because there are 140 teachers at this college, but I'm the only Deaf and African-American here. In fact, there are only two African-American teachers on campus."

Laurene enjoys her work at WOU. She knows how important it is for deaf children to have skilled teachers. She feels that the education of deaf children has improved, but she says, "We still have a long way to go!"

There are many new problems and challenges in education today. Here are some of the **major** problems for both deaf and hearing students:

1. Drug and alcohol **abuse**
2. Troubled families
3. Too much television
4. **Peer pressure**

Laurene Gallimore never sits on the side lines and watches others. She is a doer. She makes things happen because of her energy and love and her vision to make the world a better place. She has received many awards for her services to deaf people.

When she is not working to improve the lives of deaf and hard-of-hearing children, she enjoys many **hobbies**. She loves jogging, reading, poetry, and **classic** movies. Laurene is currently working on her Ph.D. at the University of Arizona. She and her husband, Max, live in South Salem, Oregon, and they have three grown college children.

The More You Know

These are some great moments in the history of the education of deaf children.

1814 Thomas H. Gallaudet meets Alice Cogswell, a young deaf girl.

1815 Thomas H. Gallaudet leaves for Europe to find ways to teach deaf children.

1816 Thomas H. Gallaudet returns to America with a young deaf teacher from France named Laurent Clerc.

1817 The first permanent school for the deaf opens in Hartford, Connecticut. It is now called the American School for the Deaf.

1864 Gallaudet College, the first college for deaf students in America, opens. It is now called Gallaudet University.

1887 The first deaf African-American teachers are hired to teach at a school for deaf children in Texas.

1988 I. King Jordan becomes the first deaf President of Gallaudet University.

Check Your Understanding

1. How do you think Laurene felt when her teachers punished her for using signs?

2. When did Laurene graduate from high school?

3. What are some major problems for students at your school?

4. Where did Laurene Gallimore grow up?

5. Do you think being deaf is a challenge or punishment?

6. If you could change something about your school, what would it be?

Write About

Write about your favorite teacher. Explain why he or she is a good role model.

Learn More About It

Danny Delcambre: The Ragin Cajun

Write to:
 The Ragin Cajun, 1523 First Ave., Seattle, WA 98101

Ken Glickman: "Prof. Glick"

Read more:
 Ken Glickman, DEAFinitions for Signlets
 (Maryland: 1986)
  and
 Ken Glickman, More DEAFinitions! (Maryland: 1989)

Books, posters, videotapes and information available at:
 DEAFinitely Yours Studio
 9201 Long Branch Parkway
 Silver Spring, MD 20901-3642
 http://www.deafology.com

Bethany "Buffy" Hummel: The Pioneer

Write to:
 Women's National Basketball Association (WNBA)
 645 5th Ave., New York, NY 10022
  or
 American Basketball League (ABL)
 1900 Embarcadero Rd., Suite 110
 Palo Alto, CA 94303

Dr. Robert Davila: The Diplomat

Read more:
Stuart Low, Democrat and Chronicle (1996)

Write to:
Rochester Institute of Technology
National Technical Institute for the Deaf
Marketing Communications Dept.
Rochester, NY 14623-5604

Laurene Gallimore: The Challenge

Read more:
Jack R. Gannon, Deaf Heritage
(Silver Spring, MD: National Association of the Deaf,
1981)

Notes

Notes